THE NFL FUN BOOK

SCHOLASTIC INC.

New York Toronto London Auckland Sydney Tokyo

Editors:
Bill Barron, Jim Natal
Art Director:
Glen Iwasaki
Designer:
Laurel Burden
Associate Editors:
Larry Eldridge, Chuck Garrity, Beau Riffenburgh
Production Staff:
Violet Lee, Louise Payne, Sandy Sumida
Contributing Writer:
Adam Sachs
Editorial Administrative Assistant:
Ellen Galloway

Illustrators: *Dave Bhang 26-31, 68-69;
Randy Chewning 12-13, 40-41, 70-71.*
Photographers: *Tom Albert 10a; Allen's Studio 54; Tim
Alexander 34a; Bill Amatucci 33b; Arthur Anderson 36a, 53b;
Rolf Benirschke 18-23; John Biever 38b, 61a; Vernon Biever
58b, 65a; David Boss 33a, 47, 51b, 57, 58a, 59a, b, 60a, 61b,
62a, 63a, 64a; Greg Cava 73b; Thomas J. Croke 51a, 74a;
Dave Cross 48a; Gin Ellis 75a; Malcolm Emmons 36c, 39a, 55a;
Emmons and Brockaway 46; Nate Fine 51a; Larry D. Fullerton
48b, 49b, 56a; George Gellatly 34b; Pete J. Groh 6a, 11a, 56c;
Rod Hanna 8b; Jocelyn Hinsen 75b; Ron Kuntz 53a; David
Liam Kyle 5b, 55b, 56b; Los Angeles Rams Cheerleaders 74b,
Tak Makita 60b; Mike Maicher 8a; John McDonough 5a; Al Mes-
serschmidt 10b, 11b, 52b; Peter Read Miller 5c, 37a; Bill Mount
73a; Darryl Norenberg 32a; Russ Reed 4a, 65b; George Ro-
barge 32b; Manny Rubio 6b, 9a, 35c, 62b, 72; Carl Skalak 38a
Robert Shaver 36b; Robert L. Smith 35a; Chuck Solomon 7a;
Jay Spencer 63b; Vic Stein 65c; Tony Tomsic 9b; Corky Tre-
win 14-15; Herb Weitman 35b, 49a, 50b; Michael Zagaris 9c, 52a.*

ISBN 0-590-33460-3

12   11   10   9   8   7   6   5   4   3   2   56789/8

Printed in the U.S.A.   28

CONTENTS

NFL Autograph Album

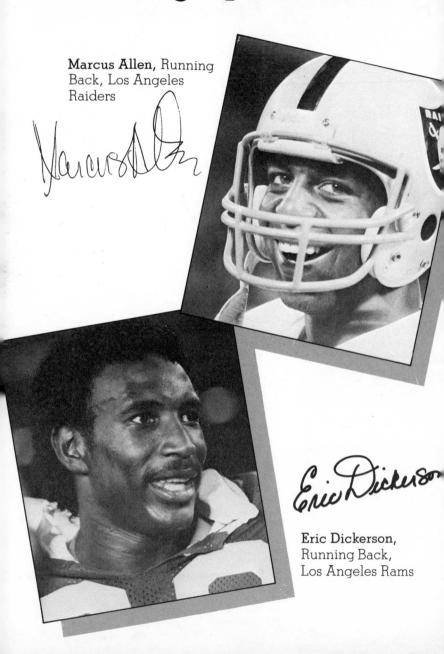

Marcus Allen, Running Back, Los Angeles Raiders

Eric Dickerson, Running Back, Los Angeles Rams

Mike Singletary,
Linebacker,
Chicago Bears

Michael Singletary

Mark Gastineau,
Defensive End,
New York Jets

Mark Gastineau #99

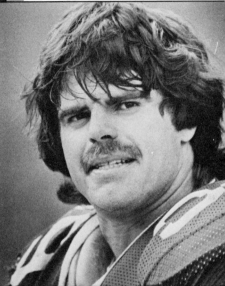

Everson Walls

Everson Walls,
Cornerback,
Dallas Cowboys

5

Chip Banks, Linebacke[r]
Cleveland Browns

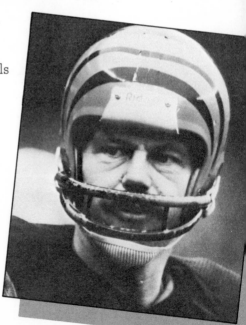

Ken Anderson,
Quarterback,
Cincinnati Bengals

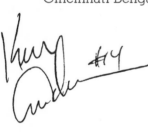

Ali Haji-Sheikh, Kicker,
New York Giants

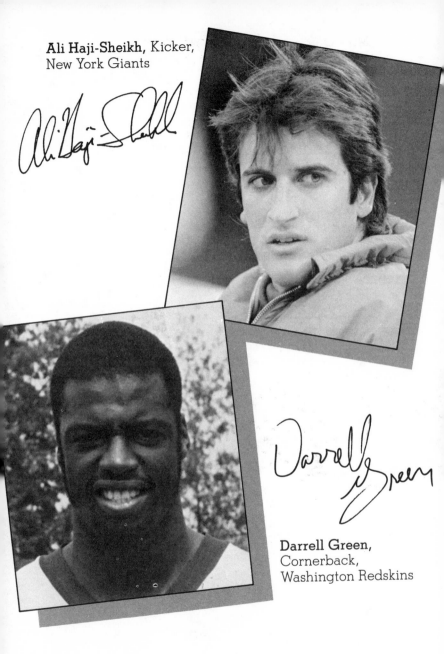

Darrell Green,
Cornerback,
Washington Redskins

Mike Quick,
Wide Receiver,
Philadelphia Eagles

Mike Quick #82

Steve Watson

Steve Watson,
Wide Receiver,
Denver Broncos

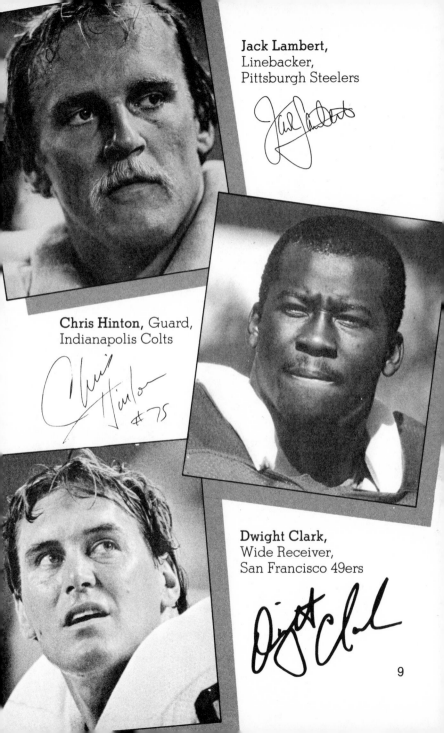

Jack Lambert,
Linebacker,
Pittsburgh Steelers

Chris Hinton, Guard,
Indianapolis Colts

Dwight Clark,
Wide Receiver,
San Francisco 49ers

9

Doug English, Defensive Tackle, Detroit Lions

Doug English

Tony Collins, Running Back, New England Patriots

Curt Warner, Running
Back, Seattle Seahawks

Curt Warner
#28

Dan Marino
#13

Dan Marino,
Quarterback,
Miami Dolphins

BIG EATERS

During training camp, players and plates are full.

It takes a lot of food to satisfy a hungry NFL football team. If you think you get hungry sometimes, how about football players who have to practice for hours in the hot summer sun during training camp? Those men are huge, and they work up appetites to match.

Take, for example, the Tampa Bay Buccaneers. In just two dinners at training camp last year, the team ate 77 pounds of beef, 27 pounds of fish, 25 pounds of fried chicken, 5 gallons of vegetable soup, 13 pounds of macaroni and cheese, 60 baked potatoes, 10 pounds of mashed potatoes, 5 gallons of gravy, 4 pounds of sour cream, 10 pounds of cottage cheese, 15 pounds of green beans, 10 pounds of cauliflower, 30 pounds of bananas, 24 pounds of grapes, 36 plums, 48 nectarines, 40 apples, 12 oranges, 2 watermelons, 200 cookies, a large chocolate cake, and a large coconut cake. And that was just for *two meals!*

How about this for just *one* Buccaneers' breakfast: 10 gallons of milk, 4 gallons of orange juice, 20 dozen (240) eggs, 5 pounds of grits, 10 pounds of corned beef hash, 15 pounds of bacon, 9 pounds of sausage, 8 pounds of hash brown potatoes, 5 pounds of cottage cheese, 4 pounds of butter, and assorted fresh fruits.

Those numbers are amazing —until you see what the Houston Oilers went through in one month at last year's training camp. In all, the Oilers players ate 3,379 pounds of beef, 431 chickens, 160 pounds of shrimp, and 2,400 pounds (1⅕ *tons,* or 80 pounds a day) of fresh fruit.

The idea of NFL players eating so much fits right in with a joke former Baltimore Colts Hall of Fame tackle Art Donovan once made about himself. "I'm a light eater," he said. "I start to eat as soon as it's light."

Which Photos Match?

Only two of the five photos shown here match. They all may look the same, but four of them have something that makes them different. Which two photos are *exactly* the same? The answer is in the Answers section.

1

2

3

4

5

NFL Position Quiz

See if you can correctly label all the player positions for the offense and defense in the diagram below. Use the list of player positions for clues (there's one position name on the list for each player on the field), then write in the correct position name beside each player. The correct answers are in the Answers section.

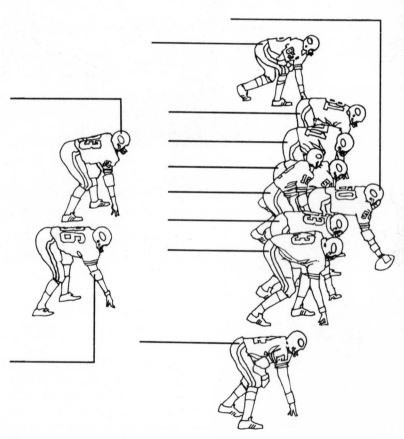

Offense

Running back	Tackle
Running back	Tackle
Quarterback	Guard
Wide receiver	Guard
Wide receiver	Center
Tight end	

Defense

Defensive end	Linebacker
Defensive end	Cornerback
Defensive tackle	Cornerback
Defensive tackle	Safety
Linebacker	Safety
Linebacker	

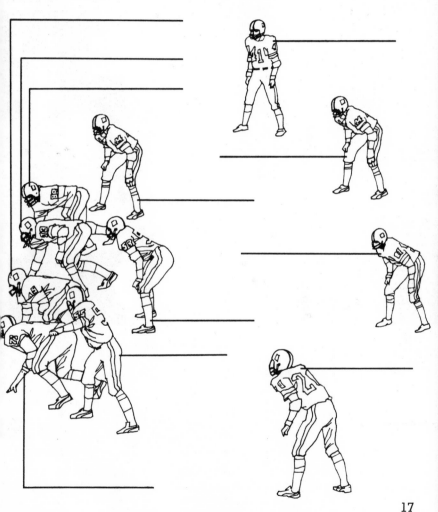

On Safari With Rolf Benirschke

Rolf Benirschke loves animals. All his life the San Diego Chargers' kicker has studied them and worked around them.

"You can say that animals have been a family affair," says the 30-year-old Benirschke, who is the NFL's third-most accurate kicker of all time

Chargers kicker Rolf Benirschke led a three-week safari through Kenya.

Rolf gets to know an African elephant on a first-hand basis.

going into the 1985 season. Rolf has scored on 71 percent of his kicks in his eight-year career. His father Kurt is the director of research at the world famous San Diego Zoo.

When Rolf had finished high school, he had the opportunity to go to South Africa. He went to the Wilderness Leadership School and worked on a game reserve. "It was one of the best times of my life," he says. "I got to combine learning and living the wildlife experience."

During the summers when Rolf was in college, he worked with his father at the San Diego Zoo, first helping out on research projects and, later, working on projects of his own. His favorite projects were working with eagles and other birds of prey, and with the giant Galapagos tortoises.

But he always wanted to get back to Africa, especially to see Kenya in East Africa. He got his chance in the spring of 1984. Rolf led a group of 21 people from the San Diego area through Kenya. In three weeks they covered more than 3,000 miles and visited nine different national parks and game reserves.

"The safari was great," Rolf says. "We traveled around in Land Rover jeeps and in topless vans and mini-buses. Five of the nights we slept out in

19

At a snake farm, Rolf's group got to handle dangerous snakes.

tents. The other nights we stayed in lodges on the reserves.

"Every morning we would get up at 5:45 and be on the road by 6:30. We'd look for animals until about 10 o'clock. After that, it would be too hot for the animals, who would be taking naps or hiding to stay

A cheetah guards its kill.

elephant, rhinoceros, buffalo, lion, leopard, and cheetah.

"One time, we came upon a gazelle that had just been killed by a pair of cheetahs," he says. "We watched for two hours as the cheetahs took turns, one eating, the other standing guard. The whole sky was filled with circling vultures. When the cheetahs had eaten their fill, the vultures began to drop out of the sky one by one. By the time we left, we counted sixty vultures around the kill. I know it sounds kind of gross, but it was exciting to watch. We were seeing first-hand what goes on there day-to-day."

cool. So we would go back to the lodge for breakfast, or drive to another park in time to make a second game run, which usually was between 3:30 and 7:30 in the evening."

Rolf says the trip was a big success because they got to see what he calls the "Big Six":

Another high point was when Rolf's group visited a snake farm. There they watched deadly snakes, including black mambas and green mambas, being milked

Rolf found water holes to be ideal places for watching wildlife.

Giraffe were among the dozens of kinds of animals the safari group saw.

for their venom. The venom then is used for research and for making antidote for people who are bitten by snakes.

But the highlight of the trip for Rolf was a balloon ride over Masai Mara Park in southwest Kenya near the Serengeti Plains of Tanzania.

"The country around there is spectacular," Rolf says. "It's what you think of when you think of Africa: rolling grasslands dotted with trees and herds of grazing animals. And to see it all from up in a balloon is amazing!"

Even though Rolf is a pro football player, he hasn't stopped working and caring for animals. In 1979, he founded Kicks for Critters, an organization that both helps save endangered species and makes people aware of the problems that face endangered species. Rolf donates $50 for each field goal he kicks. Then supporters of the program across the nation respond with matching donations. More than $600,000 has been raised since 1980. Much of the money goes to the research department of the San Diego Zoo, which shares the results of its work with scientists and wildlife researchers around the world.

"In San Diego we have the best zoo in the world," Rolf says. "But we need to do more than just look at animals there. We need to use the zoo's resources to help solve the problems of animals in the wild."

Rolf's Kicks for Critters program helps save endangered wildlife.

NFL MAP MATCH

Here's an NFL geography lesson. Try to match up the helmets of the 28 NFL teams with the NFL team cities shown on the map. To get you started, here's a free answer: Atlanta matches with number 23, the Falcons helmet. Can you do the rest? Check your answers in the Answers section.

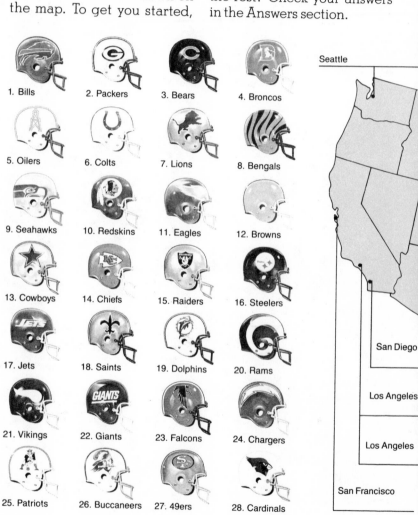

1. Bills
2. Packers
3. Bears
4. Broncos
5. Oilers
6. Colts
7. Lions
8. Bengals
9. Seahawks
10. Redskins
11. Eagles
12. Browns
13. Cowboys
14. Chiefs
15. Raiders
16. Steelers
17. Jets
18. Saints
19. Dolphins
20. Rams
21. Vikings
22. Giants
23. Falcons
24. Chargers
25. Patriots
26. Buccaneers
27. 49ers
28. Cardinals

Seattle

San Diego

Los Angeles

Los Angeles

San Francisco

Chicago

Green Bay

St. Louis

neapolis (Minnesota)

nsas City

ver

Indianapolis

Cincinnati

Detroit

Cleveland

Pittsburgh

Buffalo

Foxboro (New England)

New York

New York

Philadelphia

Washington D.C.

llas

ston

New Orleans

Atlanta

Tampa

Miami

Fun Football Dictionary

Here's your chance to learn some new and funny-sounding football words that NFL players have to use in almost every game.

AUDIBLE
A last-second change of plays shouted in code by the quarterback.

BLITZ
A preplanned but surprising pass rush involving defensive backs and/or linebackers.

BOMB
A long pass.

BOOTLEG
A trick play by the quarterback—he fakes a handoff, then hides the ball against his hip, and runs around one of the ends.

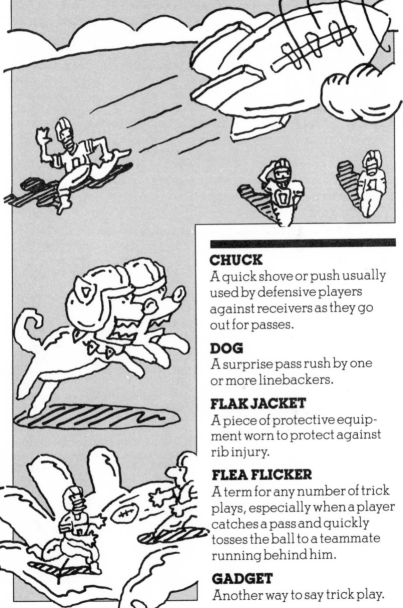

CHUCK
A quick shove or push usually used by defensive players against receivers as they go out for passes.

DOG
A surprise pass rush by one or more linebackers.

FLAK JACKET
A piece of protective equipment worn to protect against rib injury.

FLEA FLICKER
A term for any number of trick plays, especially when a player catches a pass and quickly tosses the ball to a teammate running behind him.

GADGET
Another way to say trick play.

27

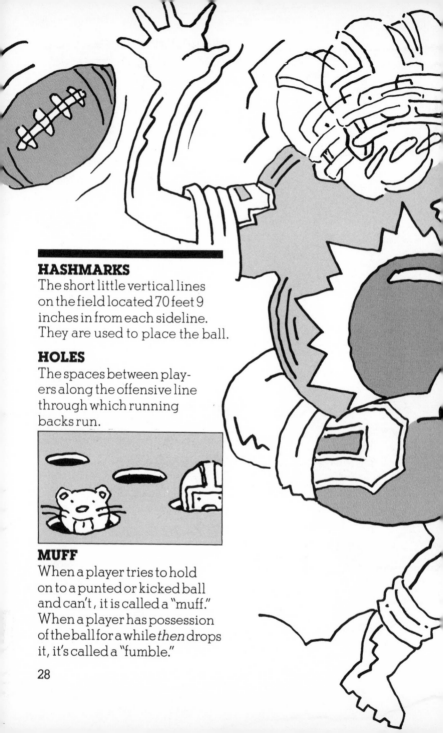

HASHMARKS

The short little vertical lines on the field located 70 feet 9 inches in from each sideline. They are used to place the ball.

HOLES

The spaces between players along the offensive line through which running backs run.

MUFF

When a player tries to hold on to a punted or kicked ball and can't, it is called a "muff." When a player has possession of the ball for a while *then* drops it, it's called a "fumble."

28

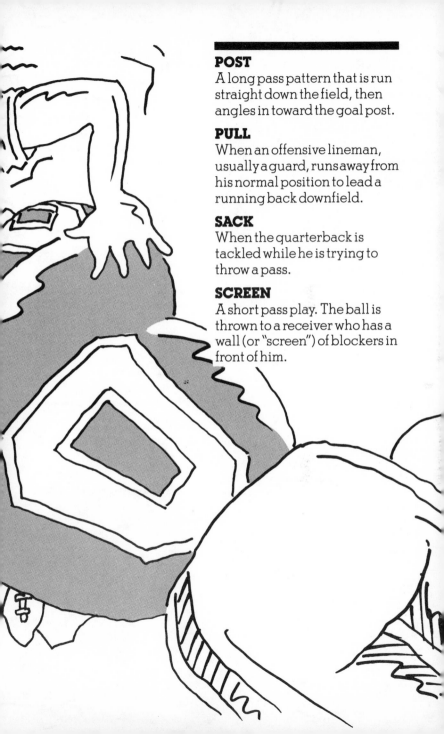

POST
A long pass pattern that is run straight down the field, then angles in toward the goal post.

PULL
When an offensive lineman, usually a guard, runs away from his normal position to lead a running back downfield.

SACK
When the quarterback is tackled while he is trying to throw a pass.

SCREEN
A short pass play. The ball is thrown to a receiver who has a wall (or "screen") of blockers in front of him.

SHOTGUN

An offensive formation where the quarterback stands five to seven yards behind the line and takes a backward pass from the center.

SNAP

The backward pass from the center that begins a play.

SPIKE

When a player slams the ball to the ground after scoring.

SQUIB

A kickoff that purposely is kicked low and bounces along the field; it is very hard to handle.

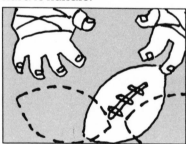

STUNT

A trick rush by linemen and/or linebackers in which they loop around each other instead of charging straight ahead. Sometimes called a "game."

SWEEP

A wide run around end.

ZONE

A special part of the field that a defensive player must protect against passes.

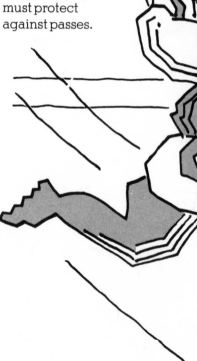

30

Fast Starters

The NFL's 1,000-Yard Rookies

Not even the best NFL running backs have been able to gain 1,000 yards every season they have played. That makes it all the more remarkable when a runner in his first NFL season hits the magic 1,000-yard mark. So far, only 19 players in NFL history have gained 1,000 yards as rookies. Here's a gallery of those very special runners.

GREG BELL, Buffalo Bills, 1984, 1,100 Yards—Bell had many injuries as a player at Notre Dame. But when he got to the NFL, he injured defenses with seven touchdowns, including one for 85 yards, the season's longest touchdown run.

ERIC DICKERSON, Los Angeles Rams, 1983, 1,808 Yards — Dickerson not only broke the 1,000-yard mark in his rookie season, he led the entire NFL in rushing and was voted to play in the AFC-NFC Pro Bowl.

CURT WARNER, Seattle Seahawks, 1983, 1,449 Yards — Warner became only the third Seahawks player ever voted to the Pro Bowl after his spectacular running helped Seattle get to its first AFC Championship Game.

JOE DELANEY, Kansas City Chiefs, 1981, 1,121 Yards — Delaney's promising NFL career was tragically cut short in 1983 when he drowned trying heroically to save three youngsters in a Louisiana swimming hole.

GEORGE ROGERS, New Orleans Saints, 1981, 1,674 Yards — Rogers not only led the league in his first season with the Saints, but came within one touchdown of breaking the NFL record (14) for touchdowns by rookie rushers.

BILLY SIMS, Detroit Lions, 1980, 1,303 Yards — Sims was a one-man show in his first year with the Lions. Running with great power and balance, he also nearly broke the rookie touchdown record with 13 touchdowns.

JOE CRIBBS, Buffalo Bills, 1980, 1,185 Yards — With his quick, short-burst style, Cribbs helped the Bills get to the playoffs his first two years with the team.

OTTIS ANDERSON, St. Louis Cardinals, 1979, 1,605 Yards — Anderson, nicknamed O.J. for the similarity of his running style to superstar O.J. Simpson, ran for more than 100 yards in nine games his rookie season, an incredible feat.

WILLIAM ANDREWS, Atlanta Falcons, 1979, 1,023 Yards — Since breaking the 1,000-yard mark his first year with the Falcons, Andrews has developed into one of the best and most versatile running backs in the NFL.

EARL CAMPBELL, Houston Oilers, 1978, 1,450 Yards — The tank-like Campbell started off fast, leading the league in rushing his rookie year, and then kept on going. He led the NFL for the next two years as well.

TERRY MILLER, Buffalo Bills, 1978, 1,060 Yards — Along with gaining more than 1,000 yards, Miller turned in the season's best performance by a rusher when he ran for 208 yards and two touchdowns in a game against the New York Giants.

TONY DORSETT, Dallas Cowboys, 1977, 1,007 Yards— Including his NFL rookie year, Dorsett put together an amazing string of 11 1,000-yard seasons between his junior year in high school (1971) and the finish of the 1981 NFL season. Dorsett ranks eighth on the all-time NFL rushing list going into the 1984 season.

DON WOODS, San Diego Chargers, 1974, 1,162 Yards — Woods was traded to the Chargers by the Packers just five days before the 1974 season opened. He went on to have seven 100-yard games and be named the NFL rookie of the year.

LAWRENCE McCUTCHEON, Los Angeles Rams, 1973, 1,097 Yards — McCutcheon had 1,000-yard years four of his first five seasons with the Rams. By 1980, when he was traded to Denver, he had become Los Angeles's all-time leading rusher.

FRANCO HARRIS, Pittsburgh Steelers, 1972, 1,055 Yards — Harris, a big man in his rookie season with the Steelers, becomes a bigger man in the league in 1984, when he should become the number-one rusher in NFL history. In 1983, he set a new NFL record by gaining 1,000 yards for the *eighth* time in his 12-year career.

JOHN BROCKINGTON, Green Bay Packers, 1971, 1,105 Yards — The Packers made Brockington their first choice in the NFL draft and he didn't disappoint them. Besides gaining more than 1,000 yards, he was named rookie of the year and was voted to the AFC-NFC Pro Bowl.

PAUL ROBINSON, Cincinnati Bengals, 1968, 1,023 Yards — Robinson's first year also was the first year for the Bengals. He got the new team off to a good start with his running, and was named the American Football League's rookie of the year in the process.

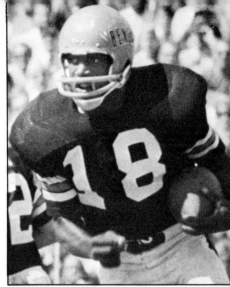

COOKIE GILCHRIST, Buffalo Bills, 1962, 1,096 Yards — In his three years with the Bills, Gilchrist ran for 3,058 yards (more than a 1,000-yard average) and scored 35 touchdowns. He also played for Denver, Miami, and in the Canadian Football League.

BEATTIE FEATHERS, Chicago Bears, 1934, 1,004 Yards — The first player to run for more than 1,000 yards in his rookie season also was the first 1,000-yard rusher in the NFL. Feathers played pro football for three more years, but never had a season to equal his first one.

WORD PILEUP

First, try to make five football words out of the five sets of mixed up letters. Then use the letters that end up in the boxes to fill in the missing word in the riddle below. The correct words and riddle answer are in the Answers section.

SAPS __ __ __ ☐

MASTUDI __ __ __ __ __ ☐ __

NUPT ☐ __ __ __

TEPLANY __ ☐ __ __ __ __ __

CRESO __ __ __ ☐ __

RIDDLE: Why are the NFL Championship Game and a red-caped comic book hero alike?

ANSWER: They both are __ __ __ __ __ .

Which Photos Match?

Are you ready to try photo matching again? See if you can pick out the two photos that are the same in the group below. Be careful! Some of the photos are pretty tricky. You can find out if you picked out the right photos in the Answers section.

Team Name Quiz

See how well you know the current 28 NFL teams. Use the team city name list for clues, then write in your answers to the questions in the spaces provided. Look for the correct answers in the Answers section.

1. How many teams have bird names? . . . . . . _____

2. How many teams have pirate mascots? . . _____

3. How many teams *don't* have their team names represented on their helmets? . . . . _____

4. How many teams have horse names? . . . . _____

5. How many teams are named after colors? . . . . _____

6. How many teams have Indian mascots? . . _____

American Football Conference

Buffalo
Cincinnati
Cleveland
Denver
Houston
Indianapolis
Kansas City
Los Angeles Raiders
Miami
New England
New York Jets
Pittsburgh
San Diego
Seattle

National Football Conference

Atlanta
Chicago
Dallas
Detroit
Green Bay
Los Angeles Rams
Minnesota
New Orleans
New York Giants
Philadelphia
St. Louis
San Francisco
Tampa Bay
Washington

The Game Must Go On

Like the Three Bears' porridge, NFL weather can be too hot or too cold; only sometimes is it just right.

Baseball games can be delayed, or called off, when it rains. But NFL games get played no matter how bad the weather is.

There have been games played during cloudbursts, when fields turned into big puddles, and players were so covered with mud that nobody could read their numbers or tell which team they were on.

There have been games played in the snow, when snowplows or people with shovels had to come out to clear off the yard lines so the teams would know where they were on the field.

And there have been games played in weather so cold there were icicles forming on the goal posts.

No NFL game ever took place in temperatures to match the 13-below-zero conditions and 15-mile-an-hour winds that the Green Bay Packers and the Dallas Cowboys had to face in the 1967 NFL Championship Game. By the time Green Bay scored a touchdown

Fans and players froze at the 1967 "Ice Bowl" game in Green Bay.

Playing in the mud is not as much fun for NFL players as for kids.

with 13 seconds left to win the game 21-17, the temperature had dropped to 26-below-zero. No wonder the game has gone down in NFL history called the "Ice Bowl"!

The weather was different, but just as bad, when the Los Angeles Rams hosted the Minnesota Vikings in the 1977 playoffs. The morning of the game, the heavens opened up over Los Angeles. The field had been covered with a tarp be-

fore the game. But as the contest went on the field turned sloppy. It got worse and worse, the players got muddier and muddier, and the ball got slipperier and slipperier. By the end of the game, neither team could do much of anything. The Vikings, who scored in the first few minutes when the field was at least playable, won 14-7. This game ended up with a nickname, too. You guessed it—the "Mud Bowl."

The San Diego Chargers got hot, then were left out in the cold, in the 1981 playoffs.

The temperature was 79 degrees with humidity to match when the Chargers beat the Miami Dolphins 41-38 in Miami. Players from both sides suffered from heat exhaustion. San Diego won on a field goal in overtime.

The next week, the Chargers had to play the Cincinnati Bengals on a sunny, but 11-degree-below-zero day in Cincinnati. The frigid weather, with a wind-chill factor of 59-below-zero, cooled off the Chargers, and the Bengals won 27-7.

The domed stadiums in the NFL, where games are played indoors, have taken away some of the weather problems teams must deal with. Still, every season probably will have a few games with weather so bad that the players will wish they would have stayed home.

The heat was too much for exhausted Chargers tight end Kellen Winslow (above) and other players in the 1981 AFC Divisional Playoff Game in Miami. The next week in Cincinnati, heat was welcome. The Bengals and Chargers used heated benches on the sidelines (right) because the temperature at game time was 11 degrees below zero.

It looks like a pool party (above), but it's a football game. When the field and the ball get wet, there are lots of fumbles, dropped passes, and puddles.

The player in the picture at the right probably wishes he could trade in his head-phones for some earmuffs as he watches from the sideline.

A snow plow played a big role in New England's victory over Miami in 1982. Kicker John Smith (left) warmed his hands as the plow cleared a space on the field. His last-minute field goal won the game 3-0 for the Patriots. The Eagles and the Cardinals were not as lucky in their game last December (below). They could have used a snow plow, but didn't have one.

In a 1982 game in a downpour at Tampa Bay (above), the Redskins and Buccaneers players needed scuba gear as much as football equipment.

Vikings defensive end Jim Marshall (left) tries to figure out what's going on in the "Mud Bowl" playoff game between Minnesota and Los Angeles in 1977.

Each NFL team or stadium has people whose jobs are to see that the playing fields are in the best possible conditions for games. But even when they do their jobs well, their work can be undone by a few hours of rain or snow (above). Sometimes the work on the fields goes on even as the game is being played (left), as in the 1982 AFC Championship Game between the Dolphins and the Jets in Miami's Orange Bowl.

Teams in cold weather cities sometimes think of bad weather as their friend, especially when it comes on the day of a game with a team from a warm weather city. The Chargers, from sunny San Diego, lost the 1981 AFC championship to the Bengals on a day so cold that Chargers quarterback (right) Dan Fouts's breath was freezing. But as more and more teams begin to play indoors in stadiums such as the Vikings' new Metrodome (below), the weather will have less and less of an effect on NFL games.

Fantastic Fans

If you think the action on the field at NFL games gets crazy sometimes, you ought to see what goes on in the stands. These fans are *really* crazy about their teams!

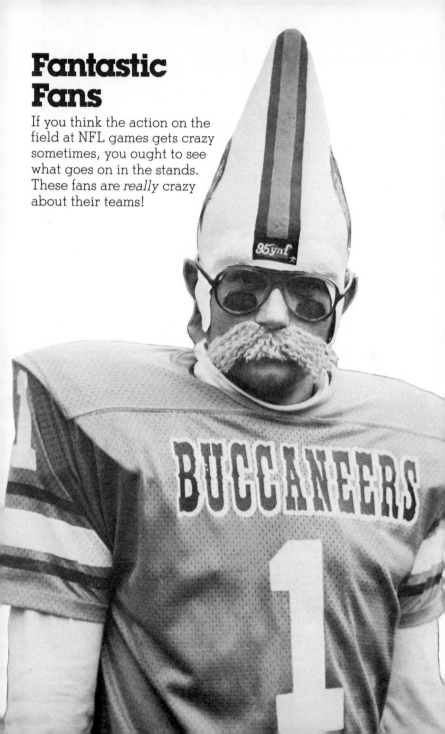

Backwards History of the Super Bowl

A Look Back at the NFL's Biggest Game, From Game XIX to Game I

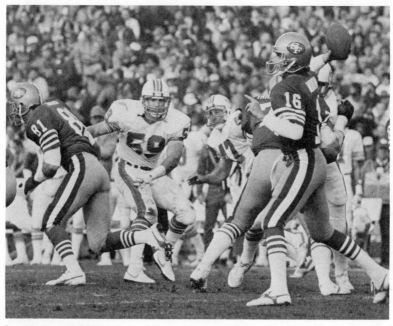

Super Bowl XIX
San Francisco 49ers 38, Miami Dolphins 16
January 20, 1985
Stanford Stadium, Stanford, California
Most Valuable Player: 49ers quarterback Joe Montana

Super Bowl XVIII ▲
Los Angeles Raiders 38, Washington Redskins 9
January 22, 1984
Tampa Stadium, Tampa, Florida
Most Valuable Player: Raiders running back Marcus Allen

◄ **Super Bowl XVII**
Washington Redskins 27,
Miami Dolphins 17
January 30, 1983
Rose Bowl, Pasadena,
California
Most Valuable Player:
Redskins running back
John Riggins

◄ Super Bowl XVI
San Francisco 49ers 26,
Cincinnati Bengals 21
January 24, 1982
Pontiac Silverdome,
Pontiac, Michigan
Most Valuable Player:
49ers quarterback
Joe Montana

Super Bowl XV ▼
Oakland Raiders 27, Philadelphia Eagles 10
January 25, 1981
Louisiana Superdome, New Orleans, Louisiana
Most Valuable Player: Raiders quarterback Jim Plunkett

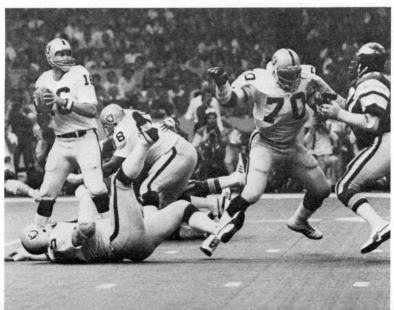

Super Bowl XIV ▲
Pittsburgh Steelers 31, Los Angeles Rams 19
January 20, 1980
Rose Bowl, Pasadena, California
Most Valuable Player: Steelers quarterback Terry Bradshaw

◄ **Super Bowl XIII**
Pittsburgh Steelers 35,
Dallas Cowboys 31
January 21, 1979
Orange Bowl,
Miami, Florida
Most Valuable Player:
Steelers quarterback
Terry Bradshaw

Super Bowl XII ►
Dallas Cowboys 27,
Denver Broncos 10
January 15, 1978
Louisiana Superdome,
New Orleans, Louisiana
Most Valuable Players:
Cowboys defensive end
Harvey Martin and
defensive tackle
Randy White

Super Bowl XI ▼
Oakland Raiders 32, Minnesota Vikings 14
January 9, 1977
Rose Bowl, Pasadena, California
Most Valuable Player: Raiders wide receiver Fred Biletnikoff

Super Bowl X ▲
Pittsburgh Steelers 21, Dallas Cowboys 17
January 18, 1976
Orange Bowl, Miami, Florida
Most Valuable Player: Steelers wide receiver Lynn Swann

◄ **Super Bowl IX**
Pittsburgh Steelers 16,
Minnesota Vikings 6
January 12, 1975
Tulane Stadium, New
Orleans, Louisiana
Most Valuable Player:
Steelers running back
Franco Harris

Super Bowl VIII ▶
Miami Dolphins 24,
Minnesota Vikings 7
January 13, 1974
Rice Stadium, Houston, Texas
Most Valuable Player:
Dolphins running back
Larry Csonka

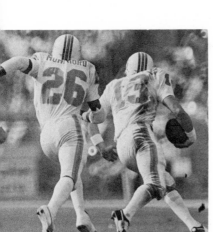

◀ Super Bowl VII
Miami Dophins 14,
Washington Redskins 7
January 14, 1973
Memorial Coliseum, Los
Angeles, California
Most Valuable Player:
Dolphins safety Jake Scott

Super Bowl VI ▶
Dallas Cowboys 24,
Miami Dolphins 3
January 16, 1972
Tulane Stadium, New
Orleans, Louisiana
Most Valuable Player:
Cowboys quarterback
Roger Staubach

◄ **Super Bowl V**
Baltimore Colts 16, Dallas Cowboys 13
January 17, 1971
Orange Bowl,
Miami, Florida
Most Valuable Player:
Cowboys linebacker
Chuck Howley

Super Bowl IV ▼
Kansas City Chiefs 23, Minnesota Vikings 7
January 11, 1970
Tulane Stadium, New Orleans, Louisiana
Most Valuable Player: Chiefs quarterback Len Dawson

◄ **Super Bowl III**
New York Jets 16,
Baltimore Colts 7
January 12, 1969
Orange Bowl,
Miami, Florida
Most Valuable Player:
Jets quarterback
Joe Namath

◄**Super Bowl II**
Green Bay Packers 33,
Oakland Raiders 14
January 14, 1968
Orange Bowl, Miami, Florida
Most Valuable Player: Packers
quarterback Bart Starr

Super Bowl I ►
Green Bay Packers 35,
Kansas City Chiefs 10
January 15, 1967
Memorial Coliseum, Los
Angeles, California
Most Valuable Player: Packers
quarterback Bart Starr

Super Bowl Rings

For scientists, the biggest prize is the Nobel. For actors, there are Oscars and Emmy awards. For writers, Pulitzers. And, for pro football players, there is no better prize than a Super Bowl championship ring.

When the 49ers' rings arrived after Super Bowl XVI, head coach Bill Walsh said, "The players were so anxious, they didn't want to wait until training camp to get them. Some players who live out of town flew into San Francisco just to pick them up."

Not all people who are given Super Bowl rings are players and coaches. Rings also go to team owners, doctors, trainers, equipment people, scouts, and front office people.

Steeler quarterback Terry Bradshaw needed all four of his Super Bowl rings so he could have one for himself. Bradshaw gave the first one from Super Bowl IX to his father, the one from Game X to his older brother, and the ring from Game XIII to a younger brother. Terry, however, wears

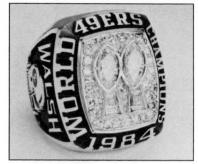

the Game XIV ring.

NFL players are big people, so their rings have to be big, too. Many Super Bowl rings weigh as much as 30 pennyweight (a jeweler's measure). That's almost four and a half times as heavy as the average high school ring. The rings given to Raider tackle Bruce Davis after Super Bowls XV and XVIII were not only heavy, they were huge. At size $20\frac{1}{2}$, (the average man's ring is size 10), they are the biggest NFL championship rings ever made—a quarter easily fits inside them!

The new 49er ring from Super Bowl XIX has a striking design. It features two raised images of the Vince Lombardi trophy (representing the 49ers' two NFL championships), with two large diamonds replacing the footballs. The trophies are surrounded by 33 more diamonds.

The Vince Lombardi Trophy

Super Bowl rings are given to players after they win the NFL championship. The Vince Lombardi Trophy is given to teams.

Designed in 1967 for Super Bowl I (the game then was called the AFL-NFL World Championship Game), it was named three years later for the great Vince Lombardi, who coached the Green Bay Packers to victories in the first two Super Bowls.

The sterling silver trophy stands 20 inches high and weighs nearly seven pounds. It is made to look like a full-size NFL football in kicking position on a tall, three-sided base. On the front of the base are the words "Vince Lombardi Trophy." Below that appear the NFL shield and the words "Super Bowl" and "AFC vs. NFC." After the game, the trophy is engraved with the names of the two teams that played and the score.

"The trophy is made of very heavy gauge silver and is very difficult to assemble and polish," says a designer for Tiffany and Company, who makes the trophy. "When we pack it for shipping we wear gloves. Then we watch the locker room celebration after the game and see everyone handling it and pouring champagne over it, and we cringe. But it's a tough, well-made piece."

STADIUM MAZE

It's the day of the big game and you have a seat on the 50-yard line. Can you find your way through the parking lot, around the stadium, and into your seat before kickoff? The correct route is shown in the Answers section.

START

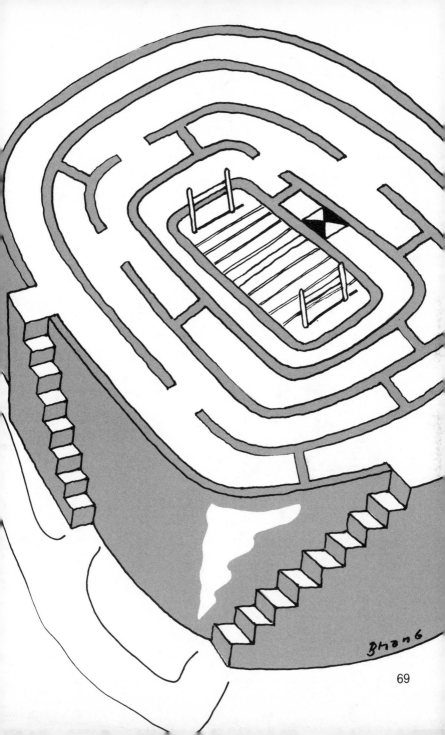

Bhang

What's Wrong Here?

There are 10 things wrong with this picture. Can you find them all? Look closely; some are easy, but some are well hidden. The complete list of all 10 is in the Answers section.

Chewning

Good Cheers

Cheering on the NFL sidelines is as much hard work as it is fun.

The Dallas Cowboys cheerleaders.

When you think of a cheerleader you probably think of a pretty girl who does a lot of high kicks, waves pom-pons, dances to music, and yells to excite the crowd. But cheerleaders do a lot more than that, especially if they cheer for an NFL team.

Take the Los Angeles Rams' cheerleading squad for example. Under the direction of Mardy Meddors, the squad works out twice a week in four-hour sessions. They practice much more than their cheers for the Rams on Sunday. Each cheerleader works on singing and voice technique, tap dancing, aerobics, and entertainment routines. They even learn about public relations, the marketing business, and how to perform in front of a camera.

Mardy calls the Rams' squad a "motivational entertainment troupe". Through hard work and practice, the cheerleaders have perfected dance and entertainment routines performed to popular hit songs. They also have worked Broad-

way show material into their program. These require longer periods of dancing and acting.

Whenever the Rams have a home game, the cheerleading squad is there to support them, but in the offseason the Rams' cheerleaders (and other NFL cheerleading squads such as the Dallas Cowboys' cheerleaders) travel all over the world. The Rams' cheerleaders put on benefit shows in many countries to entertain military families. They have performed for Americans in such places as Lebanon, Greenland, Korea, and Turkey. Mardy was surprised to find out how many people in these far away lands are football fans.

Closer to home, the cheerleaders perform at about 400 events every year for the Rams. Many outside organizations want the Rams' cheerleaders to perform for them because of their high level of talent and energy. The Rams' cheerleaders entertain and help support about 100 charity events a year, 40 NFL golf tournaments, and 100 custom design and musical fashion shows. They also do about 40 road shows at shopping malls each year to promote the Rams. It takes great spirit and energy to handle this seven-day-a-week, year-round job.

About one-third of the

The Los Angeles Rams cheerleaders.

Rams' cheerleaders are in school, about one-third work at regular jobs, and one-third are in the entertainment industry. Even so, they all are able to put maximum effort and energy into their cheerleading. They even hold clinics and training camps for high school and college squads.

The New England Patriots cheerleading squad, called the Patriots Spirits, also hold a very popular cheerleading clinic in the Boston area. Last year, more than 300 kids from ages 8 to 20, representing every New England state, attended the clinic to learn cheers and chants, dance and

A Raiders cheerleaders tryout.

pom pon routines, partner stunts and pyramids, and gymnastics. At each clinic a Miss Spirit is chosen. She gets to cheer with the Patriots Spirits at an NFL game.

The Patriots Spirits, who are very active with the Rhode Island and Massachusetts Special Olympics programs, are a bit different from most NFL cheerleading squads. They have two units: a 31-member dance unit, and a 14-member gymnastics squad, half of whom are men.

Spirits director Susan Oulette says the Spirits are very dedicated. "They want to

The New England Patriots Spirits.

The Los Angeles Rams cheerleaders entertain U.S. servicemen abroad.

The Atlanta cheerleaders add color to Falcons games.

Colts cheerleaders in the rain.

cheer, rain or shine. They're out there in the same weather as the players." She even has one cheerleader, in her fifth year with the squad, who lives in Maine and drives *three hours* one-way to make the games!

What does it take to be an NFL cheerleader?

"Intelligence, personality, stage presence, talent, and good appearance," says Oulette. "And practice. Lots of practice."

Fun Book Funny Pages

Finish the jokes, puns, and riddles below by filling in the blanks with NFL team names. If you can't figure them out, you only have to turn the page for the answers.

1. How much does corn cost in Tampa?

_____

2. What are Snoopy's favorite dogs?

B ___   ___   ___   ___   ___

3. Indiana Jones faced them in his first movie.

_____

4. Why was the cowboy always sneezing?

Because he kept catching _____.

5. What do ducks have instead of noses?

_____

6. $7 \times 7 = ?$

_____

7. What are streetcars and buses called in some cities?

T _____   _____   _____   _____

8. Places to find very hot, bubbling water.

B ___ ___ ___ ___ ___ ___

9. Beige, tan, chocolate, and mahogany are shades of

_____

10. They come out on summer lawns.

Dande _____

11. People who take things that don't belong to them are

_____

12. Cowgirls like them.

_____

Answers

Which Photos Match?
(pages 14-15)

Photos 2 and 3 match.

NFL Position Quiz
(pages 16-17)

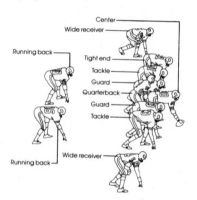

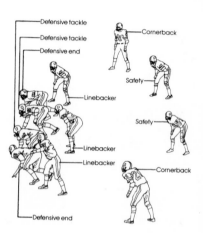

NFL Map Match
(pages 24 and 25)

Atlanta Falcons 23
Buffalo Bills 1
Chicago Bears 3
Cincinnati Bengals 8
Cleveland Browns 12
Dallas Cowboys 13
Denver Broncos 4
Detroit Lions 7
Green Bay Packers 2
Houston Oilers 5
Indianapolis Colts 6

Kansas City Chiefs 14
Los Angeles Raiders 15
Los Angeles Rams 20
Miami Dolphins 19
Minnesota Vikings 21
New England Patriots 25
New Orleans Saints 18
New York Giants 22
New York Jets 17
Philadelphia Eagles 11
Pittsburgh Steelers 16

St. Louis Cardinals 28
San Diego Chargers 24
San Francisco 49ers 27

Seattle Seahawks 9
Tampa Bay Buccaneers 26
Washington Redskins 10

Word Pileup
(pages 40-41)

PAS**S**
STADI**U**M
PUNT
P**E**NALTY
SCO**RE**

Riddle answer:
They both are **SUPER**.

Team Name Quiz
(pages 44-45)

1. **Four:** Seahawks, Falcons,
   Eagles, and Cardinals
2. **Two:** Raiders and Buccaneers
3. **One:** Browns
4. **Two:** Broncos and Colts
5. **One:** Browns
6. **Two:** Chiefs and Redskins

Which Photos Match?
(pages 42-43)

Photos 2 and 4 match.

Stadium Maze
(pages 68-69)

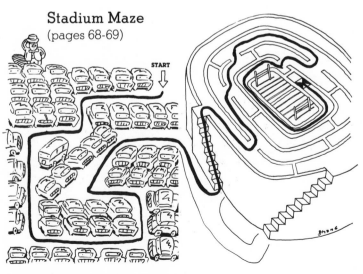

What's Wrong Here?
(pages 70-71)

1. Player number 78 isn't wearing a helmet.
2. Player number 78 isn't wearing shoes.
3. Player number 44's jersey number is backwards.
4. Player number 44 is wearing shorts.
5. Player number 44 is riding a unicycle.
6. Player number 12 is wearing a helmet with the wrong kind of facemask.
7. Player number 12 is carrying a beach ball instead of a football.
8. Player number 12 is wearing cowboy boots.
9. The referee has on a checked, instead of striped, shirt.
10. The 50-yard line is in the wrong place on the field.

Fun Book Funny Pages
(pages 76-77)

1. Buccaneers
2. Beagles
3. Raiders
4. Colts
5. Bills
6. 49ers
7. Trams
8. Boilers
9. Browns
10. Dandelions
11. Steelers
12. Cowboys